Johann Baptist Cramer

Eight-four Celebrated Studies for the Pianoforte

Johann Baptist Cramer

Eight-four Celebrated Studies for the Pianoforte

ISBN/EAN: 9783744783620

Printed in Europe, USA, Canada, Australia, Japan

Cover: Foto ©Thomas Meinert / pixelio.de

More available books at **www.hansebooks.com**

Schirmer's Library of Musical Classics

✦

Vols. 142-145

JOHANN BAPTIST CRAMER

EIGHTY-FOUR
CELEBRATED STUDIES

FOR THE

PIANOFORTE

IN FOUR BOOKS

Book I	Book III.
Studies 1-21	Studies 43-63
Book II	Book IV
Studies 22-42	Studies 64-84

BOOK I CONTAINS A BIOGRAPHICAL SKETCH OF THE AUTHOR

BY

DR. THEO. BAKER

G. SCHIRMER, INC., NEW YORK

Printed in the U.S.A.

The life of **JOHANN BAPTIST CRAMER** furnishes a striking illustration of the career of a man who, having exceptionally solid acquirements, has bequeathed to posterity his most valuable knowledge in an enduring form. Both as a professional musician and as a business-man, he enjoyed uninterrupted prosperity. Born at Mannheim, Germany, on Feb. 24, 1771, of musical German lineage—his father being a distinguished violinist, his grandfather a noted flutist—he was taken the following year to London, where his father settled permanently.

At a very tender age he manifested such decided proclivities for the pianoforte that he was allowed to make that instrument his chief study ; though his father also gave him lessons on the violin, and in harmony and theory. His best-known teachers, however, were Clementi (for a year or two) and C. F. Abel.

But Cramer's mind was of that rare order which early learns to derive more benefit from independent study and observation than from the precepts of pedagogues. Both in musical theory and in piano-playing he was essentially self-taught. In the former, the text-books of Marpurg and Kirnberger were his guides;—those were the days before learning had been made easy, and much reflection (not to say self-abnegation), and a strong gift for "reading between the lines," were needed by the student desirous of gaining clear insight into the mysteries of counterpoint. At the age of 13 he already had an enviable pianistic reputation ; at 17, his professional tours commenced, taking him to several great continental cities, and winning him well-merited praise and renown.

Up to the year 1824 his time was divided between the aforesaid tours, his work as a piano-teacher, and composition. Cramer the pianist and teacher was a prime favorite in London in both capacities. His taste, nurtured by an intelligent study of the older German classics, was wholesome and utterly free from morbidity ; his playing was brilliant, and of finished elegance ; he was a notable sight-reader, and a master of extemporization in strict contrapuntal style; in his touch, expression and power were united; especially remarked at that period was his beautiful interpretation of adagio movements; in a word, if not *primus inter pares*, he was one of the foremost pianists of his day. Cramer acquired the *cantabile* touch for which Clementi's execution was afterwards so celebrated, before the latter himself had adopted it; i. e., he thought this problem out before his master had done so; this fact should stand to his credit in the history of pianoforte-playing. His natural inclination to thoroughness in his work had cultivated, on the mechanical side, an unusually equal development of his hands. All these qualities left their combined impress on his compositions.

We may pass over the 105 Sonatas, the 7 Concertos,

and all the chamber-music, variations, fantasias, etc., etc., which have, for the most part, been cast aside by the march of modern impressionism; they belong to a by-gone era of taste and feeling. But in regard to the development of pianoforte-technique, we go back even beyond Bach; and Cramer is a later intermediate link that cannot well be dropped from the chain of evolution.

Cramer's Studies for Pianoforte are those of his works wherein the composer yet lives and labors among us. They are still looked upon as indispensable. To quote Edward Dannreuther (in Grove's Dictionary): "His [Cramer's] representative work, ' 84 Studies,' is of classical value for its intimate combination of significant musical ideas with the most instructive mechanical passages." Some students (we are sorry to say !) call Cramer's Studies *dry*. Now it is true that they, like any other Études, may be *made* so by unsympathetic treatment or superficial apprehension of their construction. But they were never intended merely for technical exercises; form and subject-matter are to be studied together with, and as integral factors in, the technical difficulties to be mastered; and careful study of their internal structure is sure to meet its reward in keen interest in, and appreciative comprehension of, the beauties which, before, lay hidden under a solidity of merit which is sometimes mistaken for heaviness.

It is easy, on examining these and the other Études which formed a part of Cramer's great Pianoforte-Method, to recognize on how firm a foundation Cramer's reputation was built; easy, too, to see that the same personal characteristics which brought such marked success to the artist, would likewise insure a high position to the man of affairs. In 1824 the publishing-house of Cramer & Co. was founded, and, thanks to the repute and energy of its head, and the popularity of his compositions, prospered from the beginning, and still flourishes.

The remainder of Cramer's life was passed between London and Paris. He withdrew from active participation in musical matters in 1845, and died on April 16th, 1858.

Cramer was on terms of intimacy with Haydn, and well acquainted with Moscheles and other leading musicians of the time. It is a matter of record, that he was the only contemporary piano-player of whom Beethoven thought well—all the rest, in the latter's estimation, amounting to nothing. This fact at least clearly establishes Cramer's claim to a command of expression and of nuance in tone uncommon among the virtuosi of the period. And the Studies, if practised in accord with the spirit in which they were written, cannot fail to be productive of good results, intellectual as well as technical, commensurate with the earnest application of the student.

THEO. BAKER

STUDIES.

BOOK I.

J. B. CRAMER.

Allegro. (♩ = 132.)

1.

f *sempre legato*

Printed in the U. S. A.

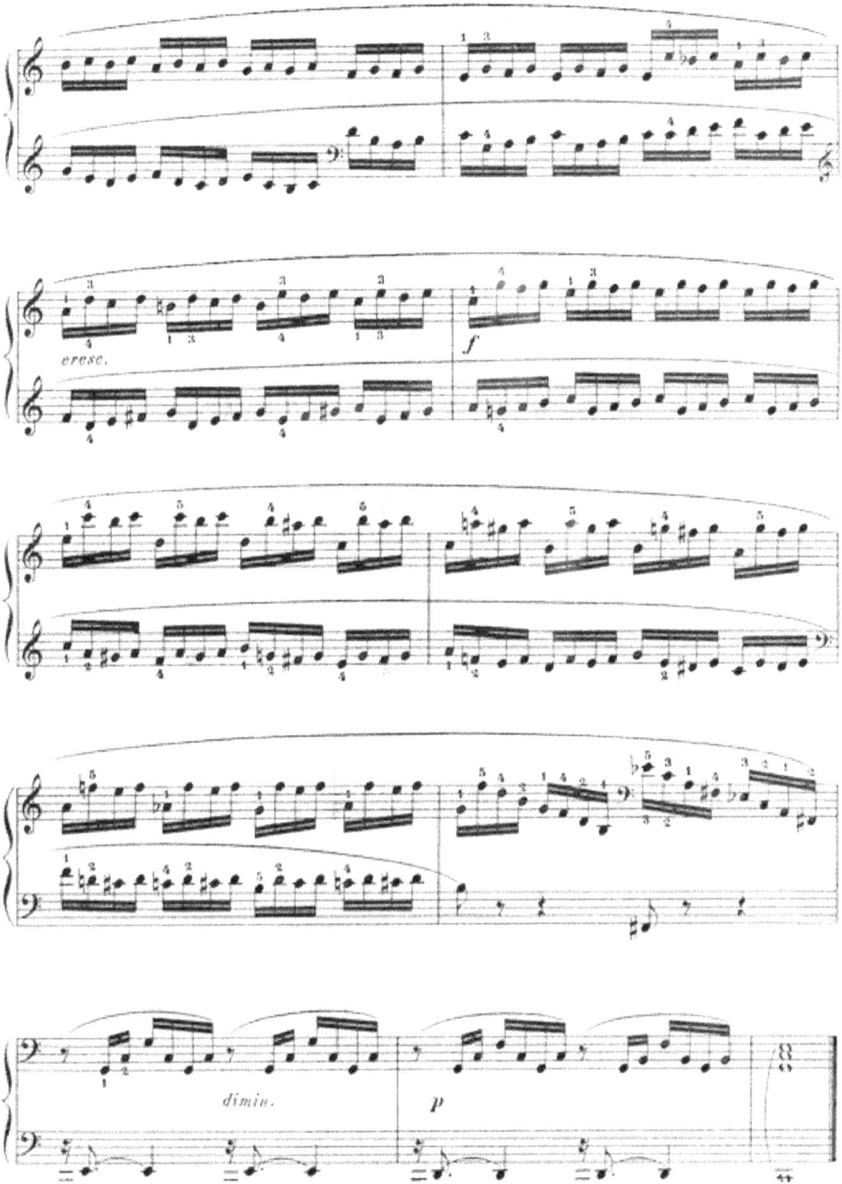
cresc.
f
dimin.
p

4

2.

Presto. (♩ = 100.)
sempre legato.

15721

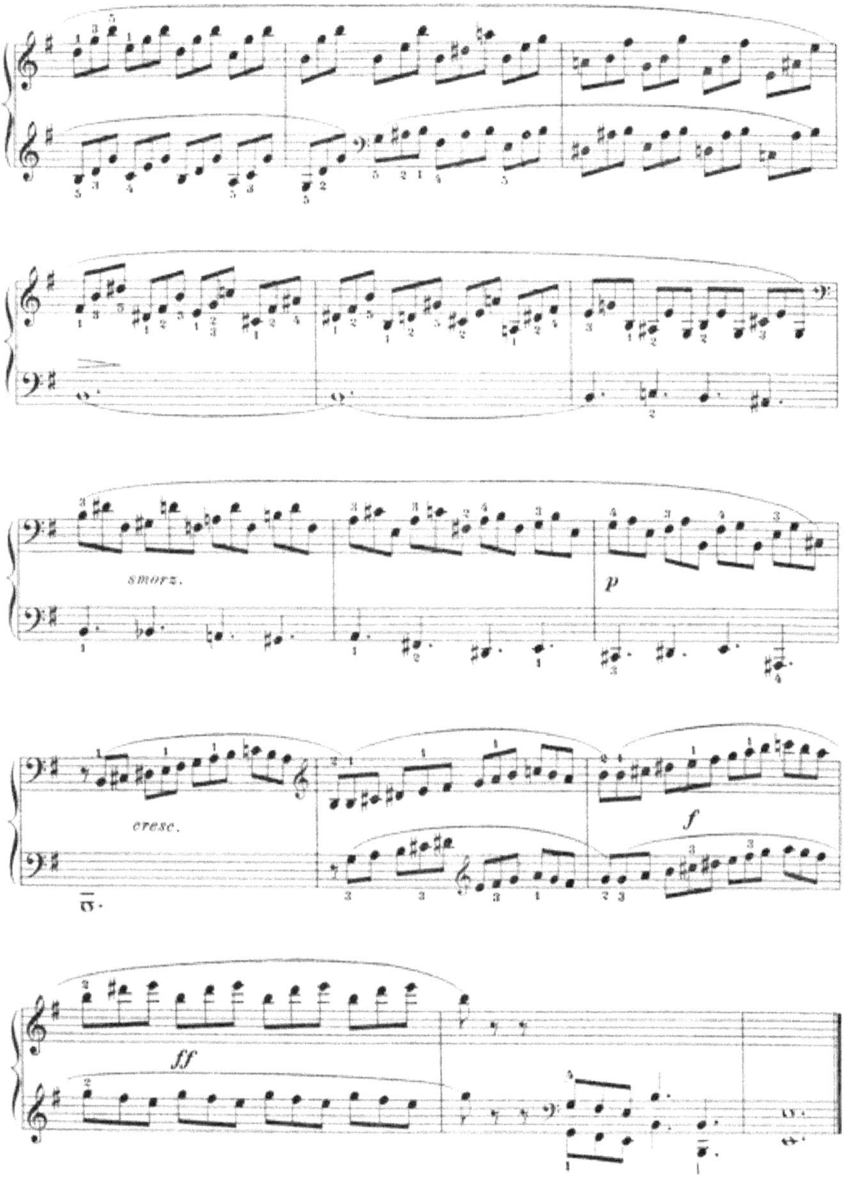
smorz.
p
cresc.
f
ff

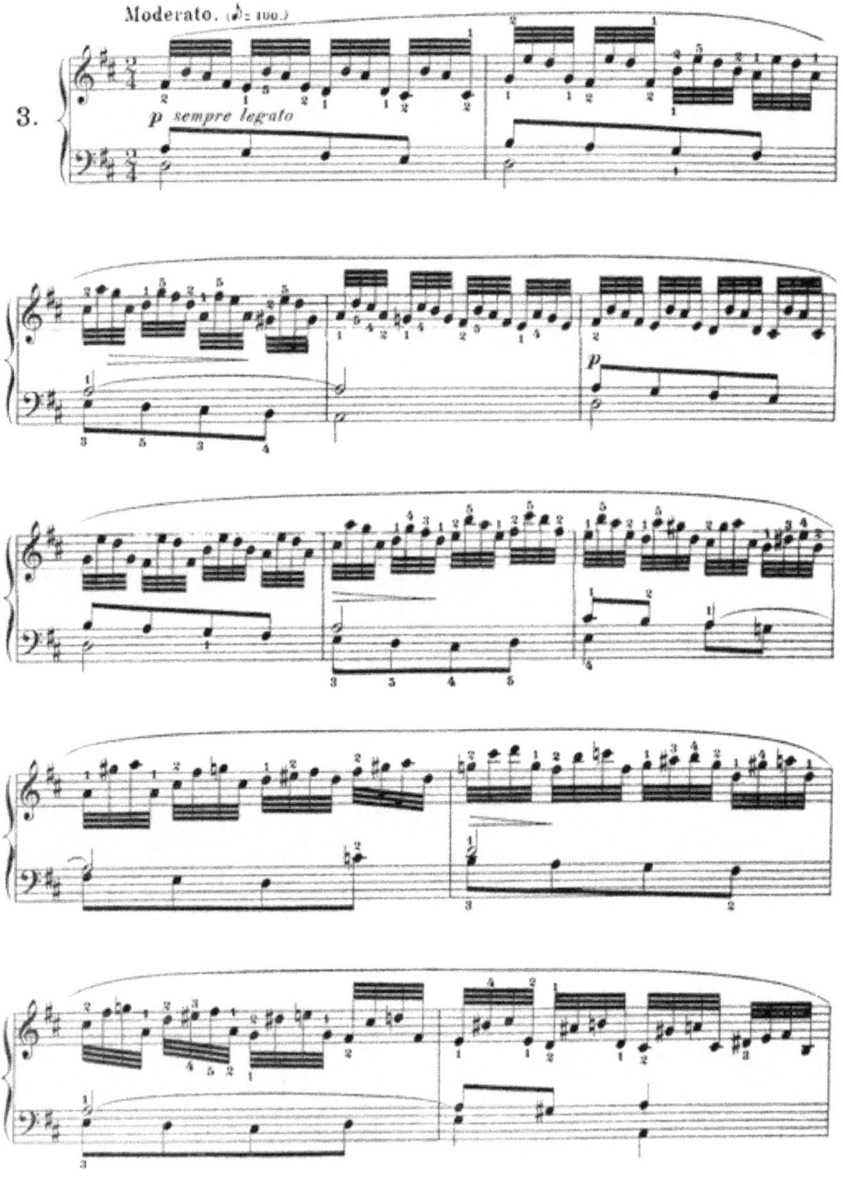

Moderato. (♪= 100.)
3.
p sempre legato
p

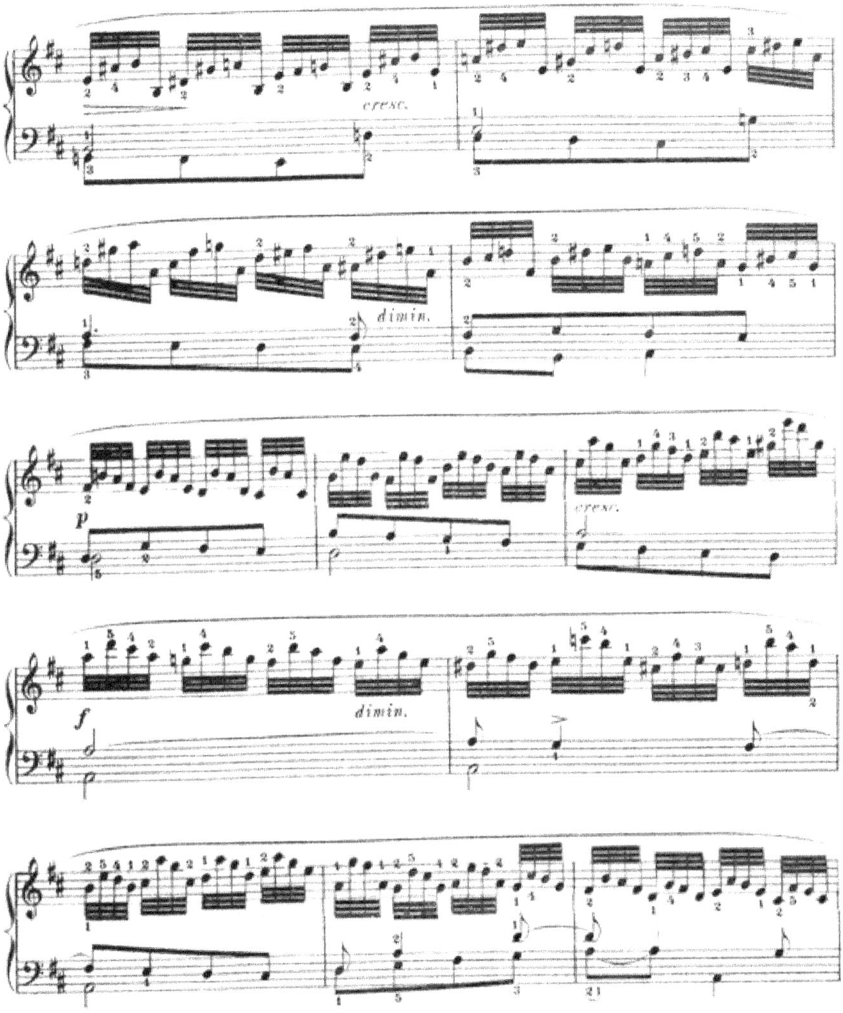
cresc.
dimin.
p
cresc.
f
dimin.
pp

Con moto. (♩ = 104)

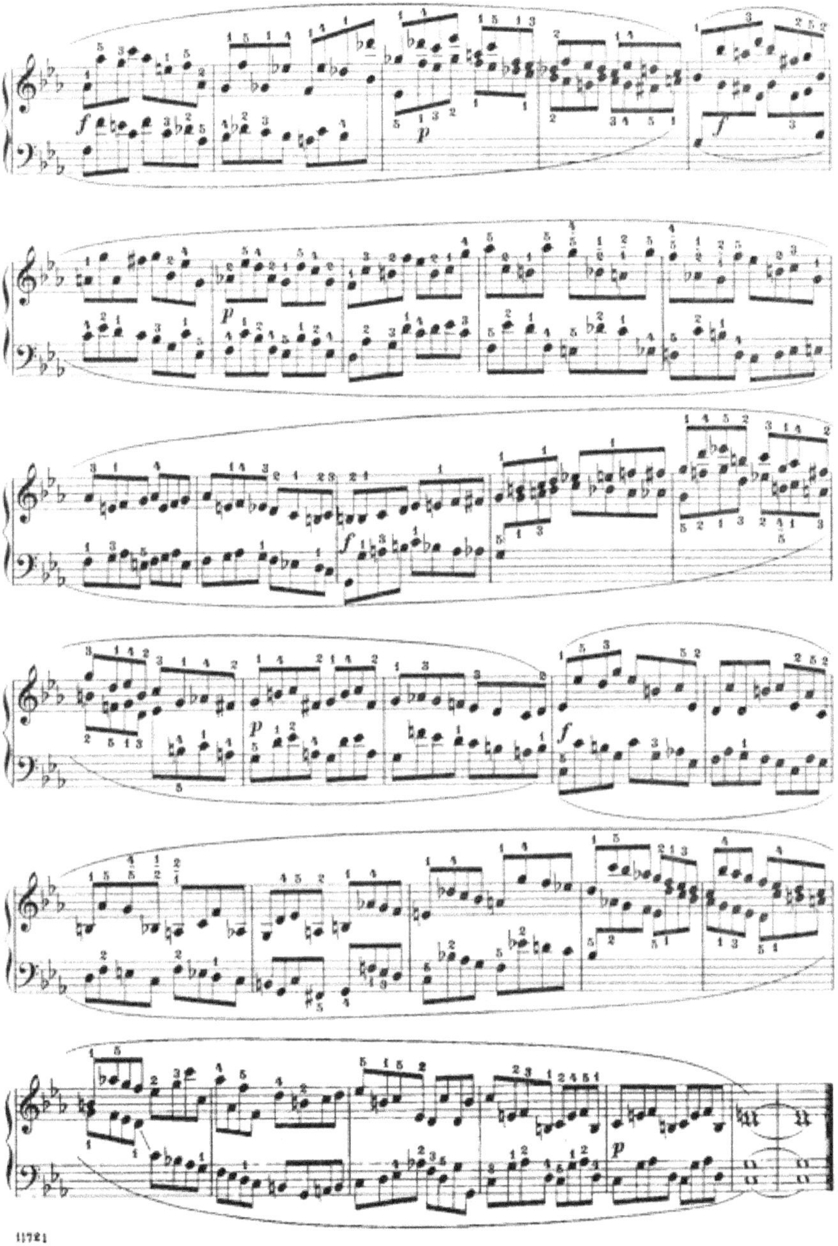

10

Allegro moderato. (♩ = 132.)

5.

11721

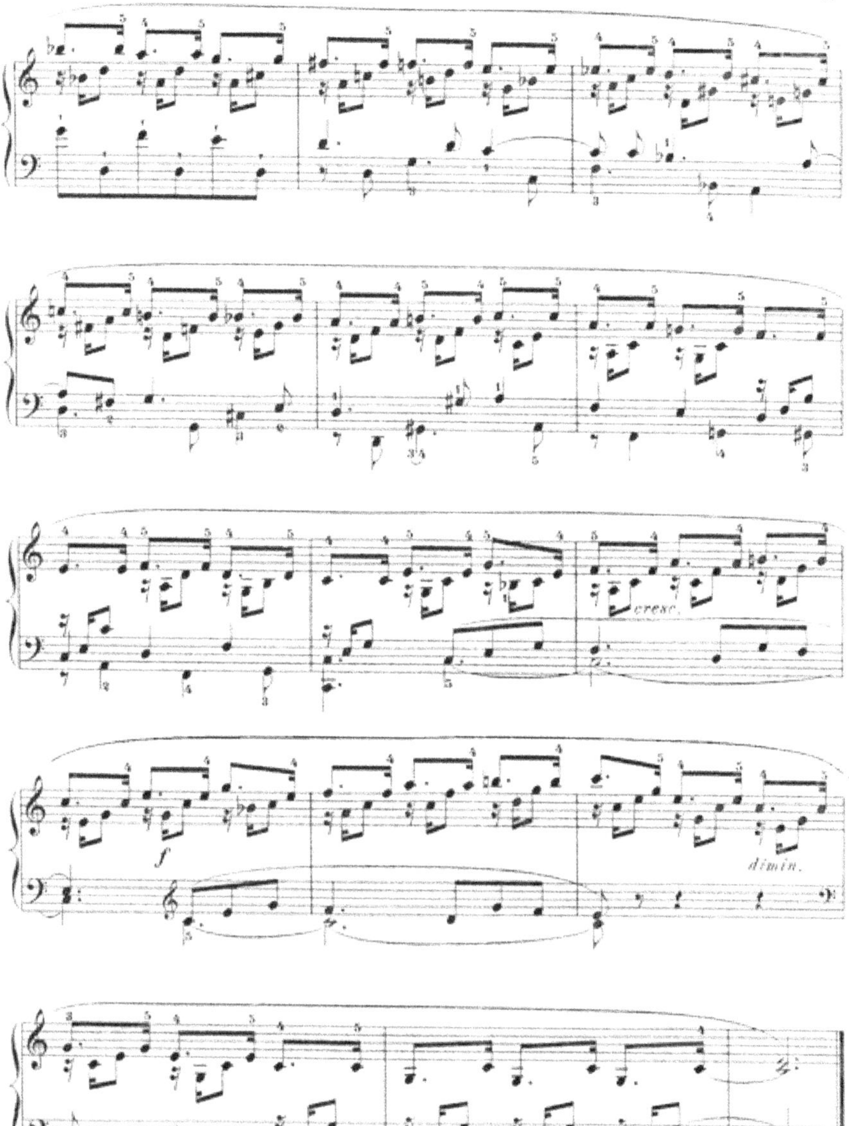
cresc.
f
dimin.

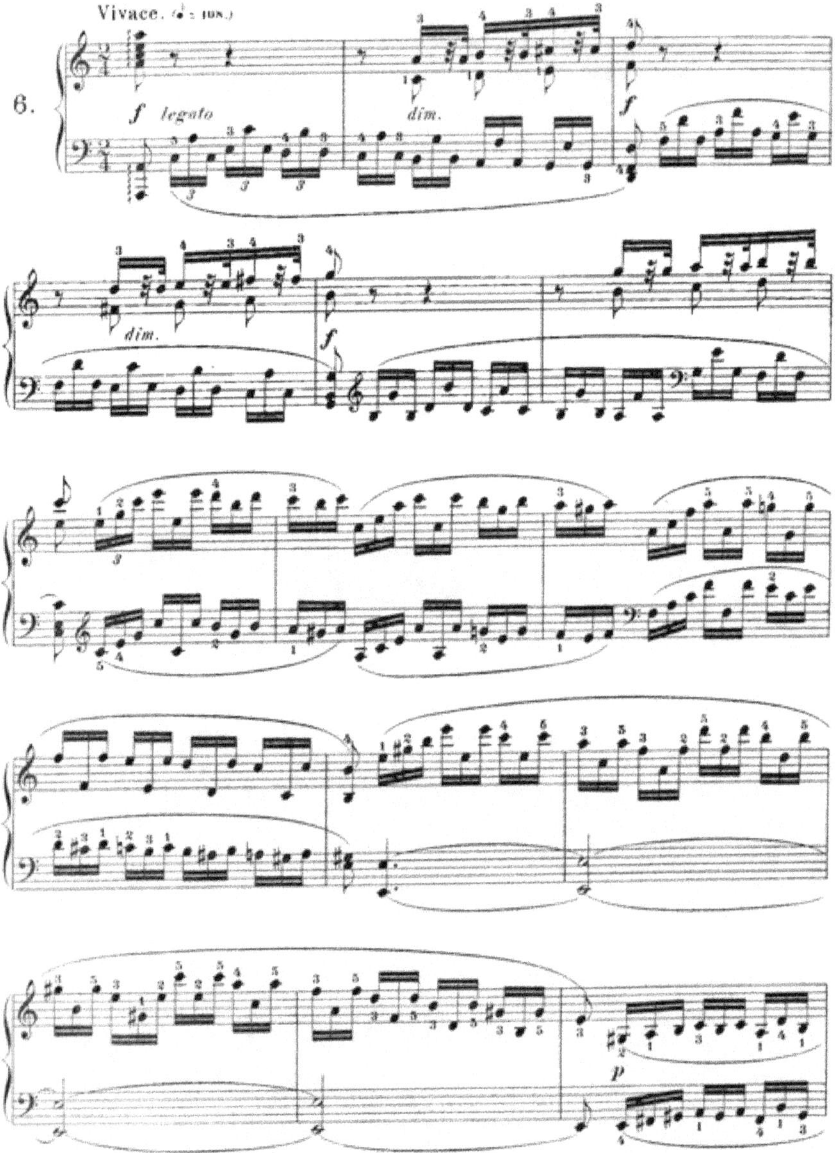
Vivace. (♩. = 108.)
6.
f legato
dim.
f
dim.
f
p

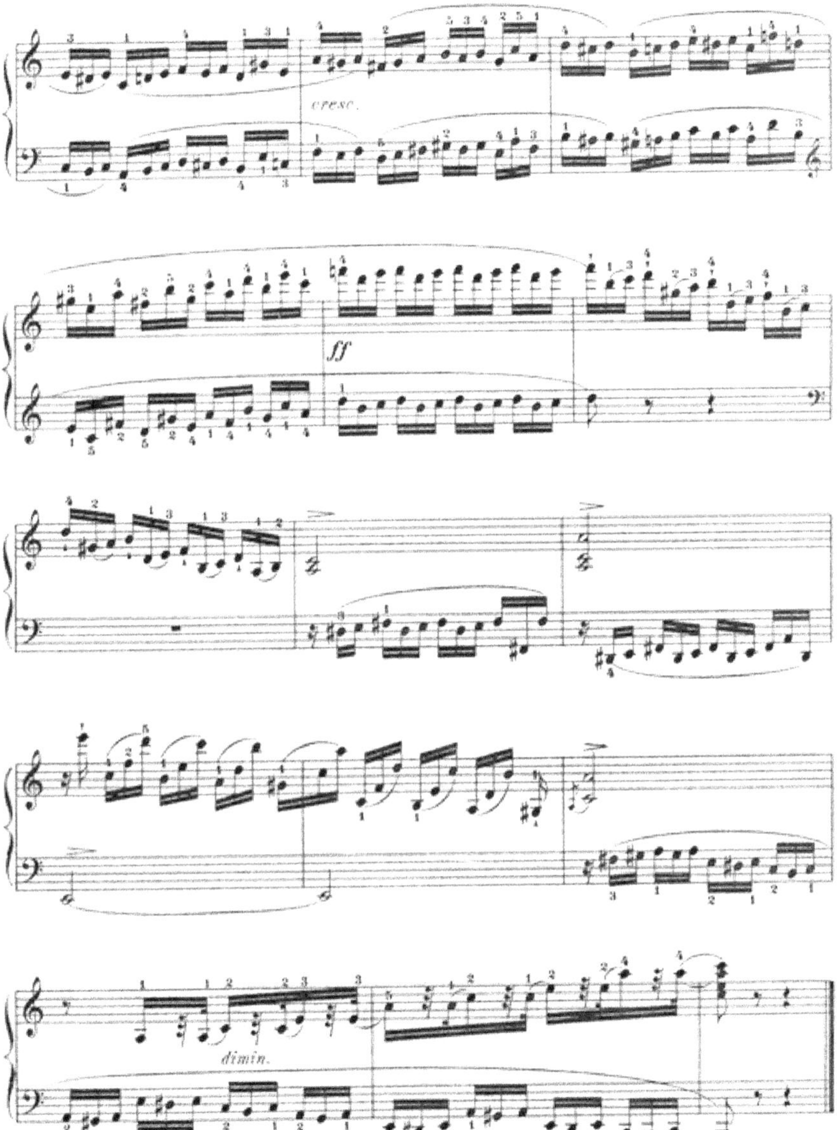
cresc.
ff
dimin.

Piuttosto moderato. (♩ = 92.)

7.

dolce e sempre legato

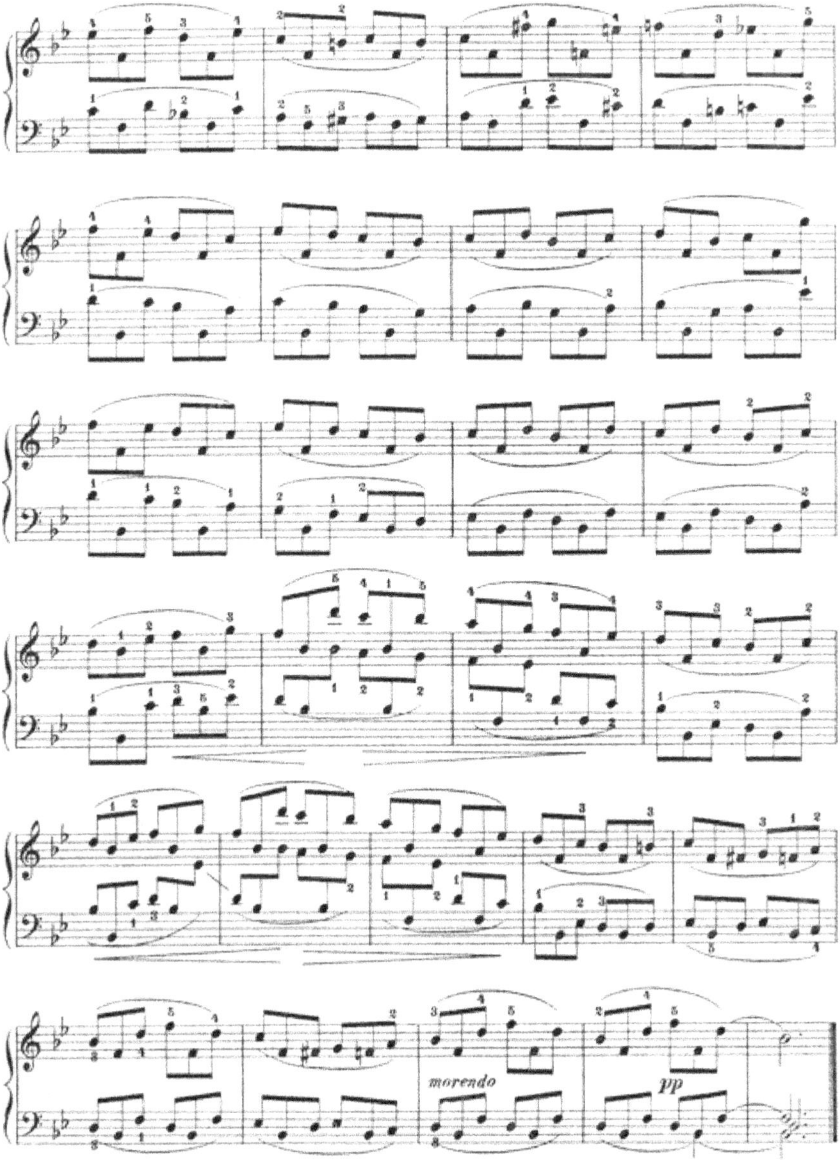
morendo
pp

16

Allegro. (♩ = 84)

8.

11721

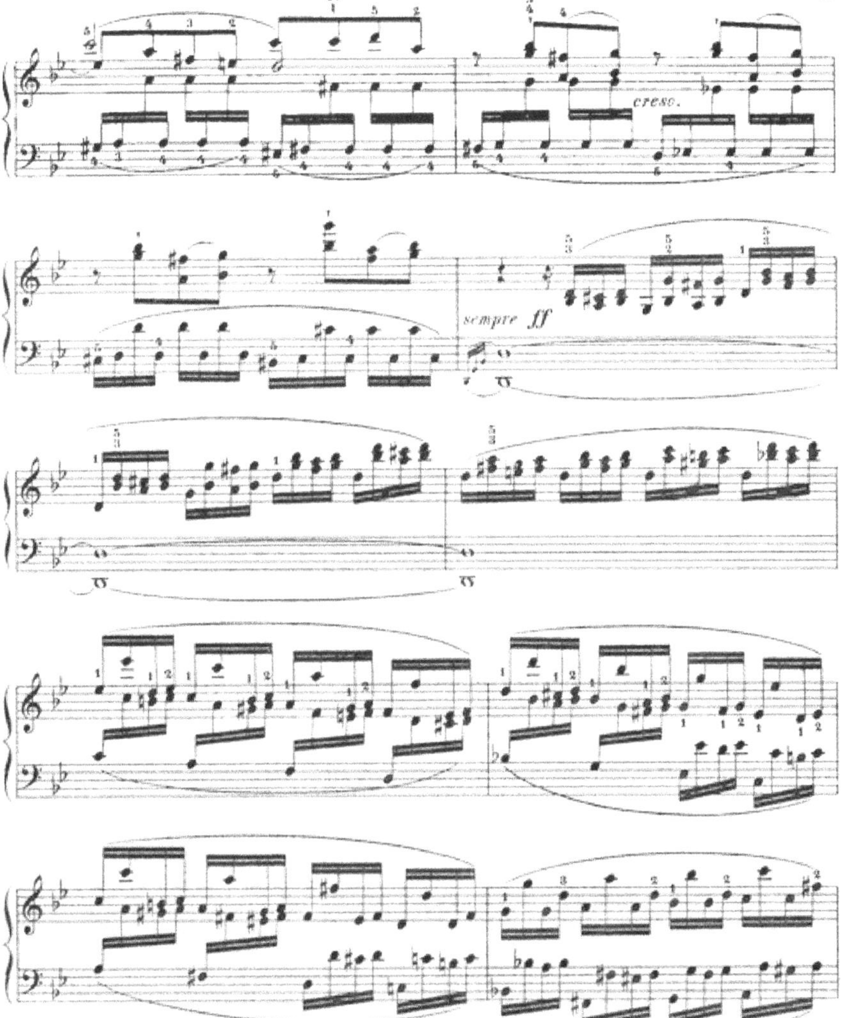
cresc.
sempre ff

Allegro moderato. (♪= 132.)

9.

p legato.

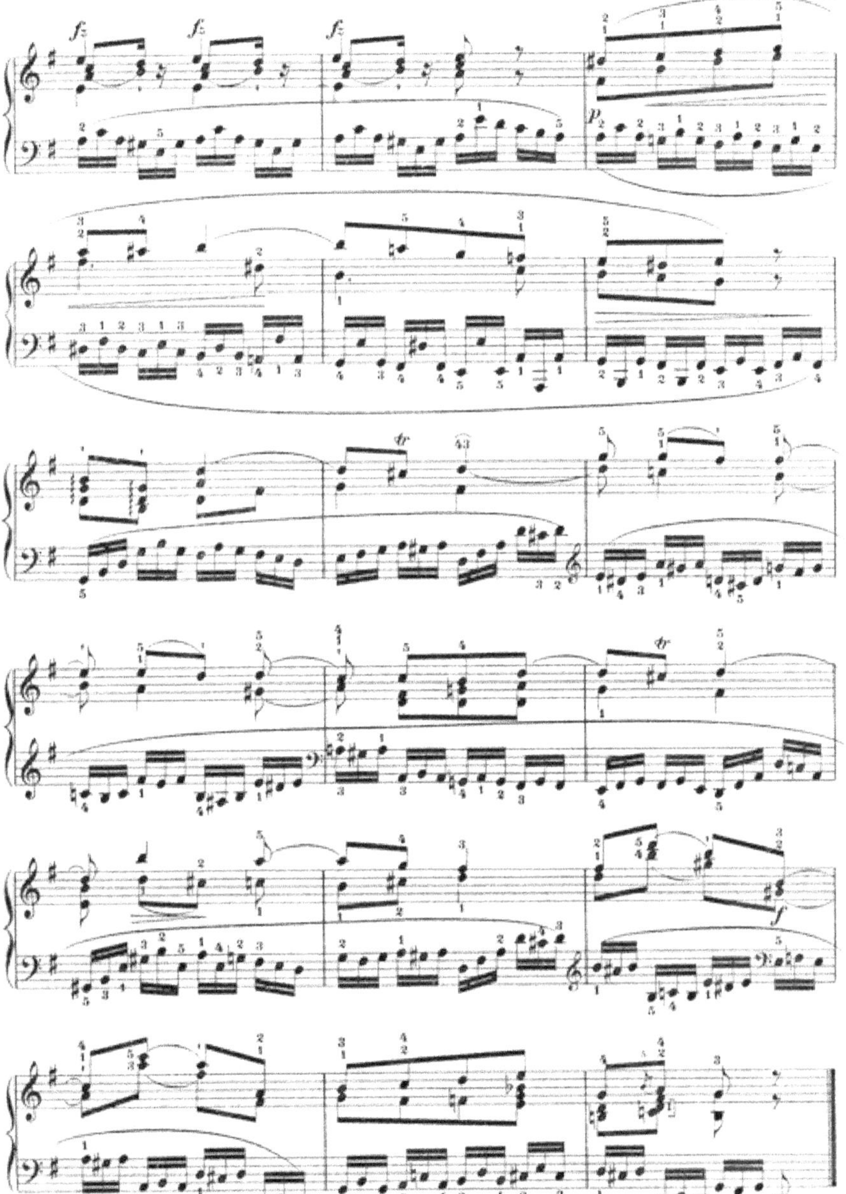

10.

Moderato. (♩. = 76)

p sempre legato.

cresc.

f

cresc.

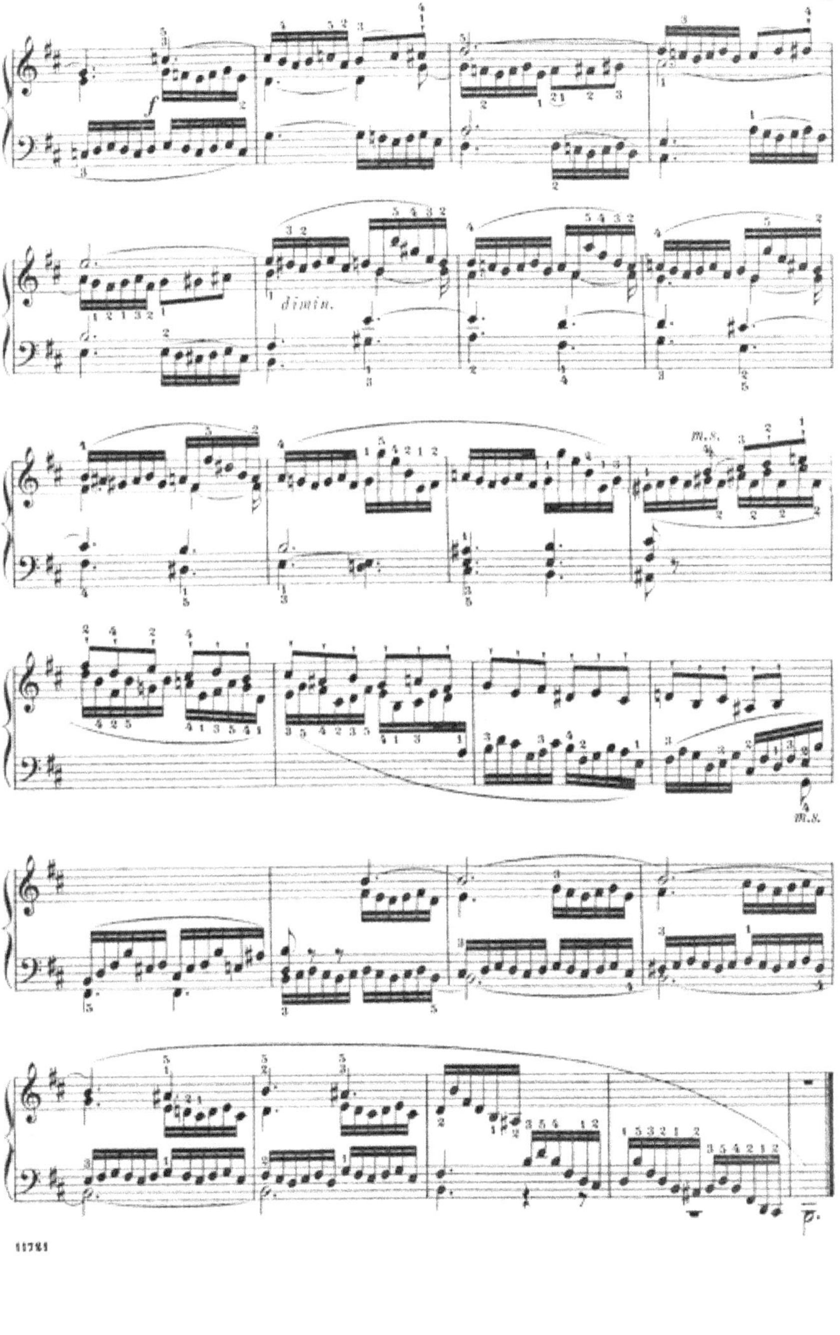
f
dimin.
m.s.
m.s.

Lento. (♩= 76)

11.

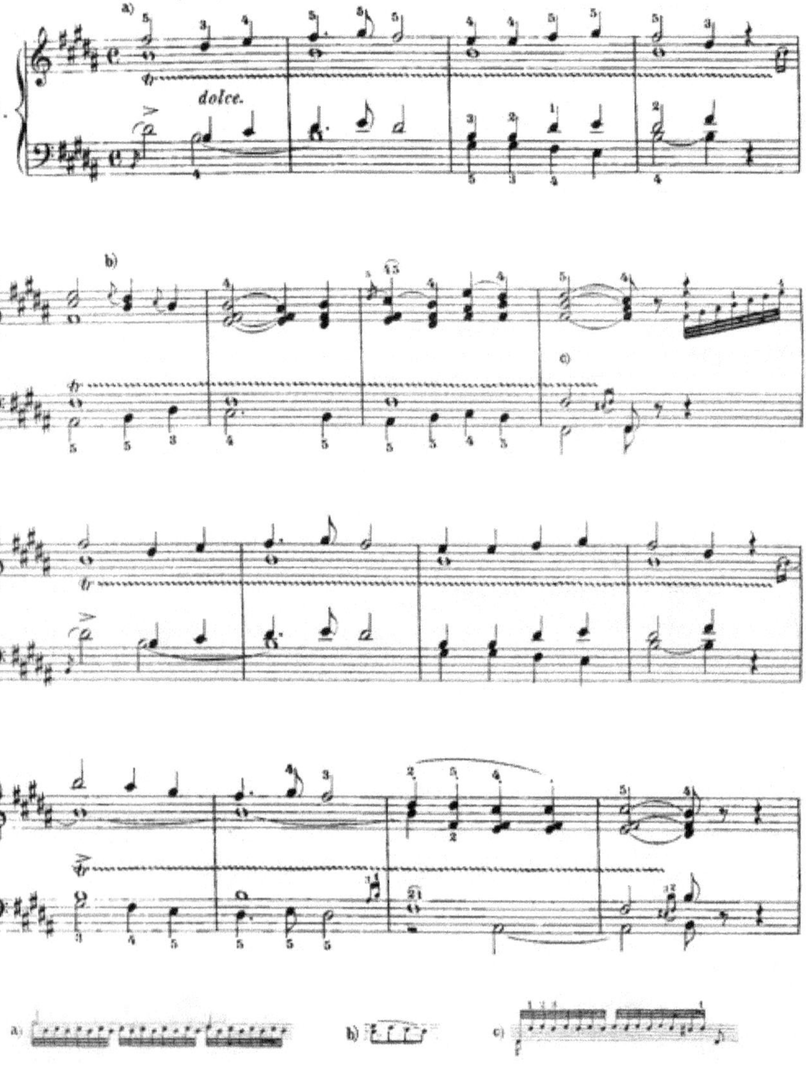

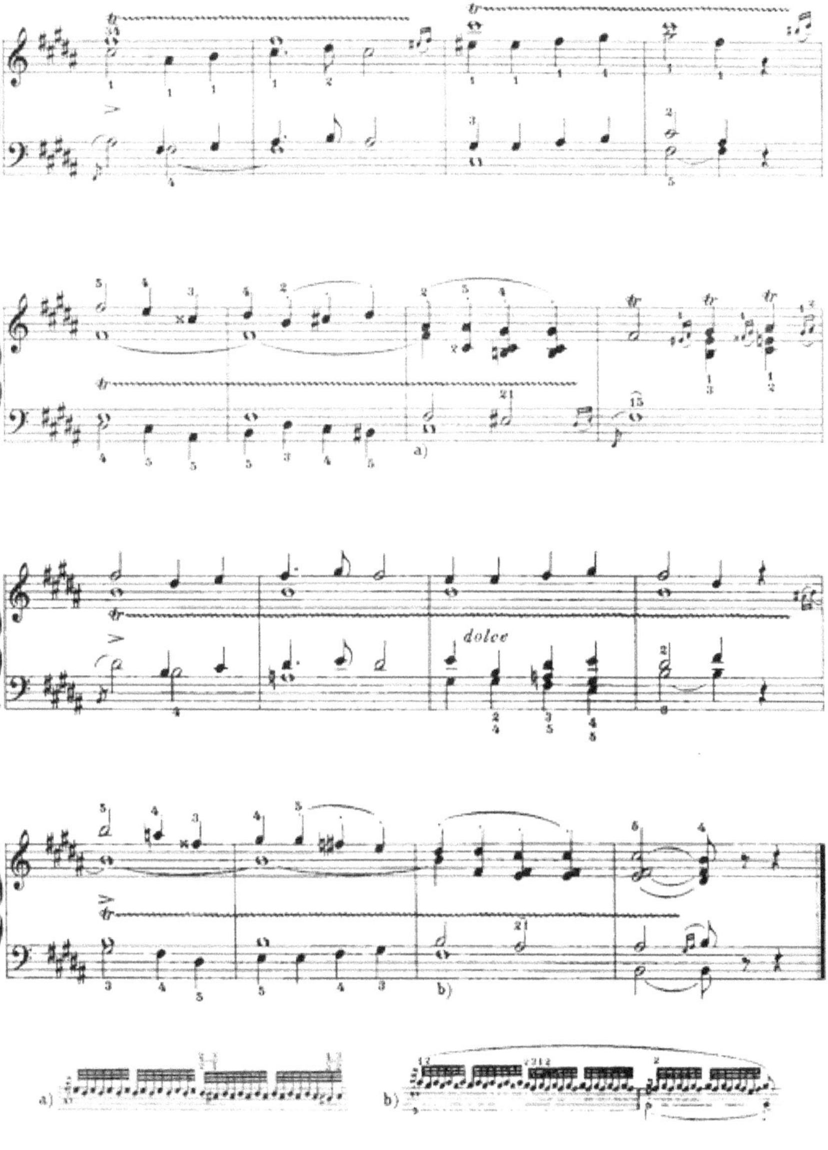
tr
dolce
a)
b)

Moderato espressivo. (♪ = 138)

12.

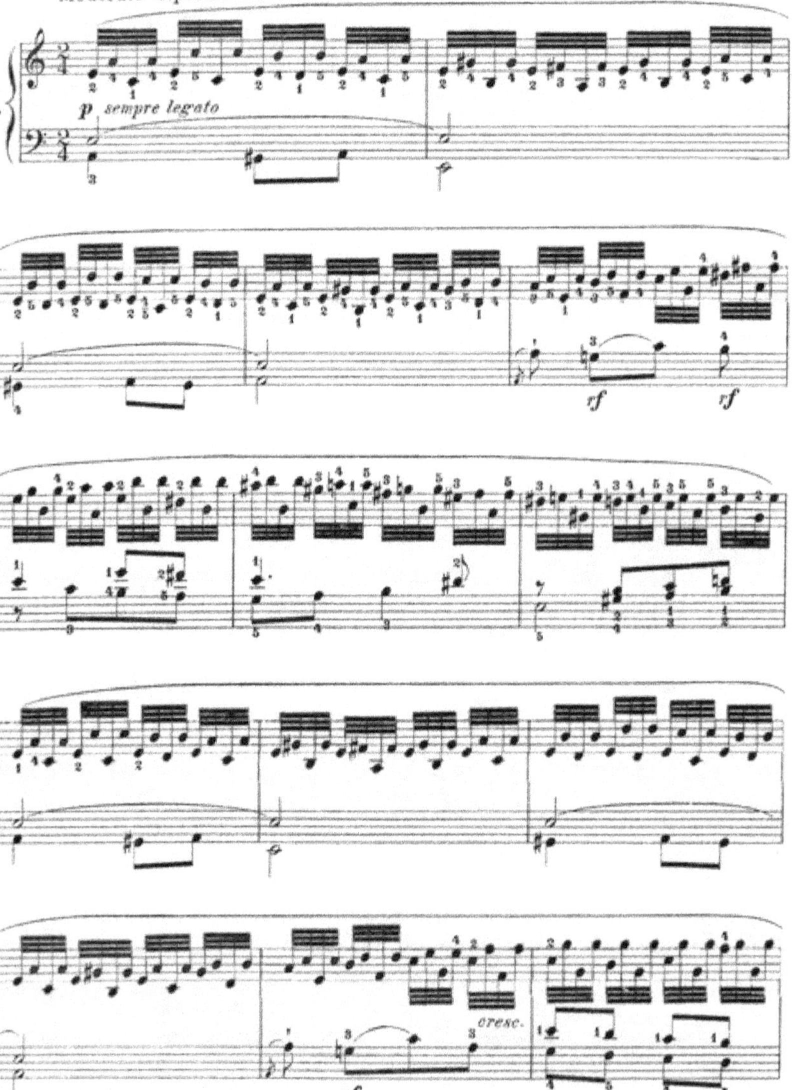
p sempre legato
rf
rf
rf
cresc.

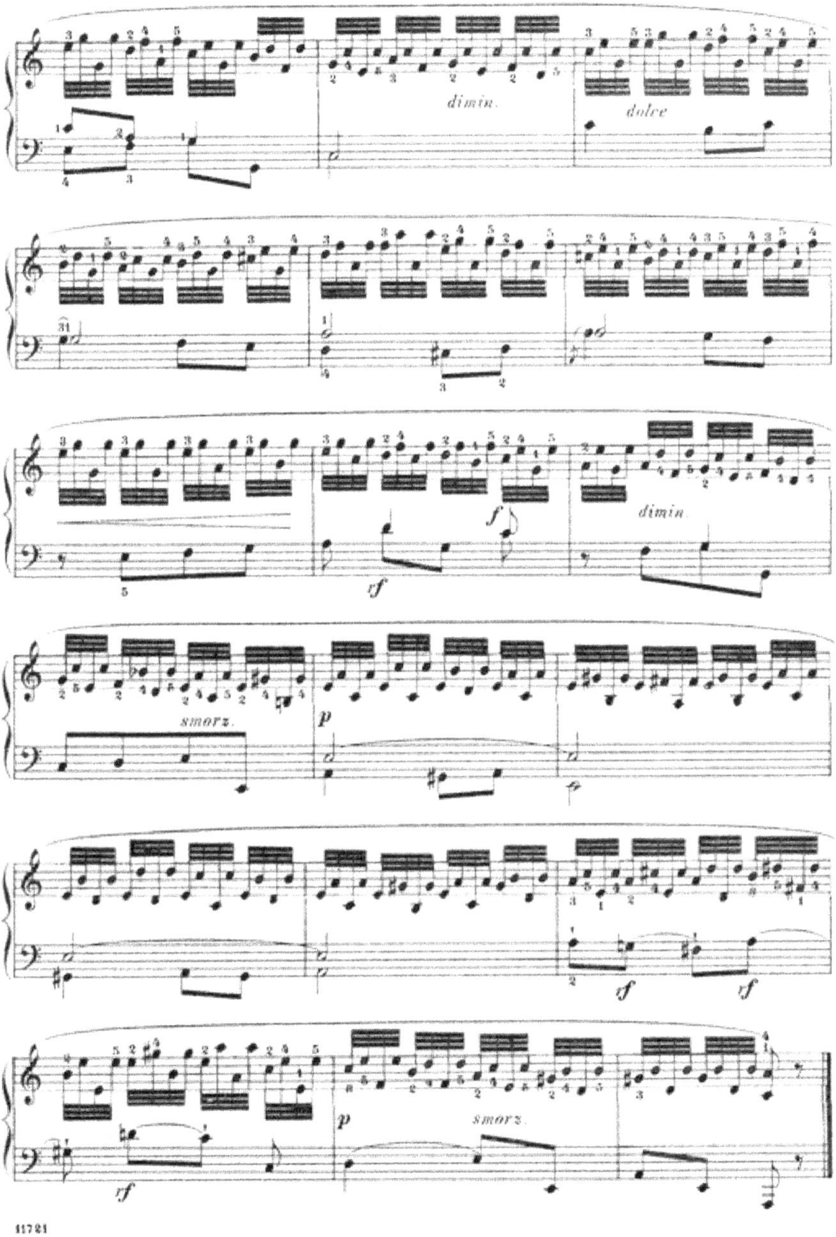
dimin.
dolce
rf
f
dimin.
smorz.
p
rf
rf
rf
p
smorz.

Spiritoso. (♩. 132.)

13.

sempre legato

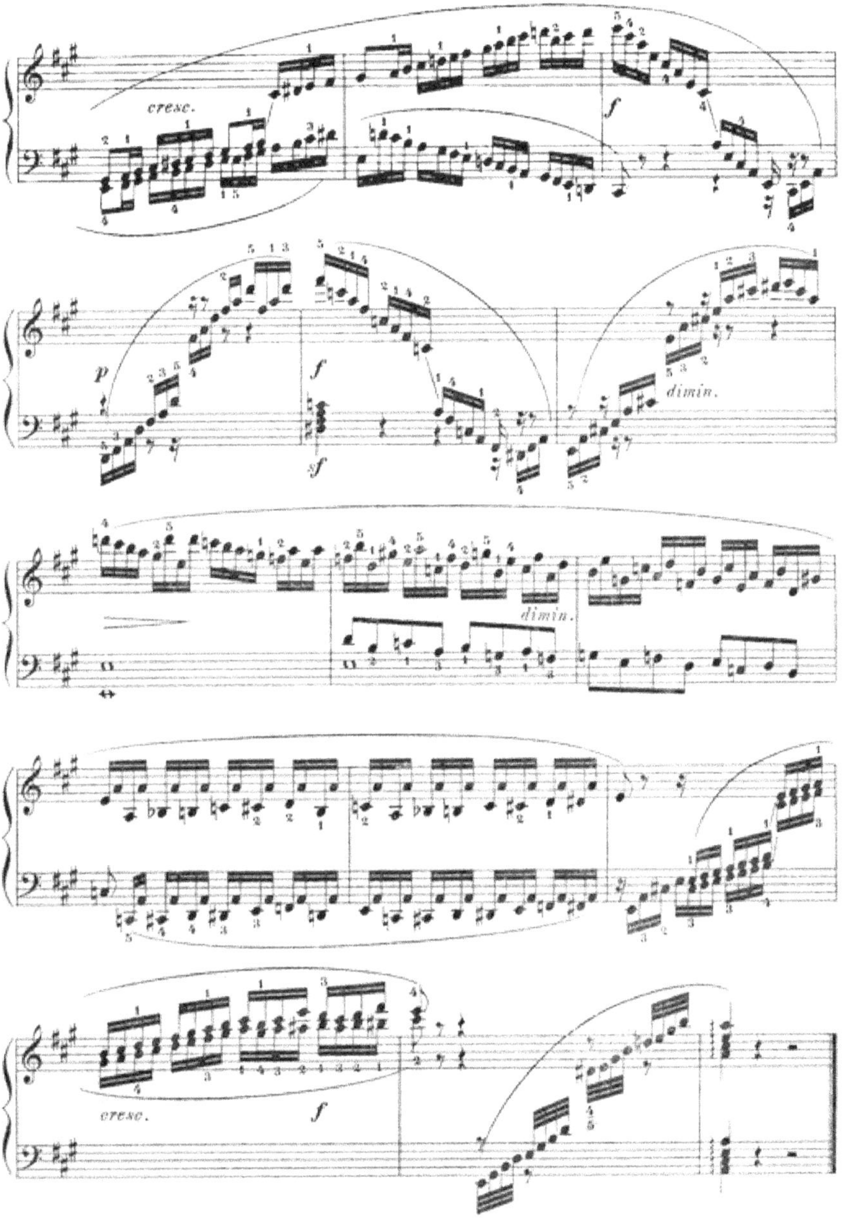
cresc.
f
p
f
sf
dimin.
dimin.
cresc.
f

Moderato.

14.

sempre legato.

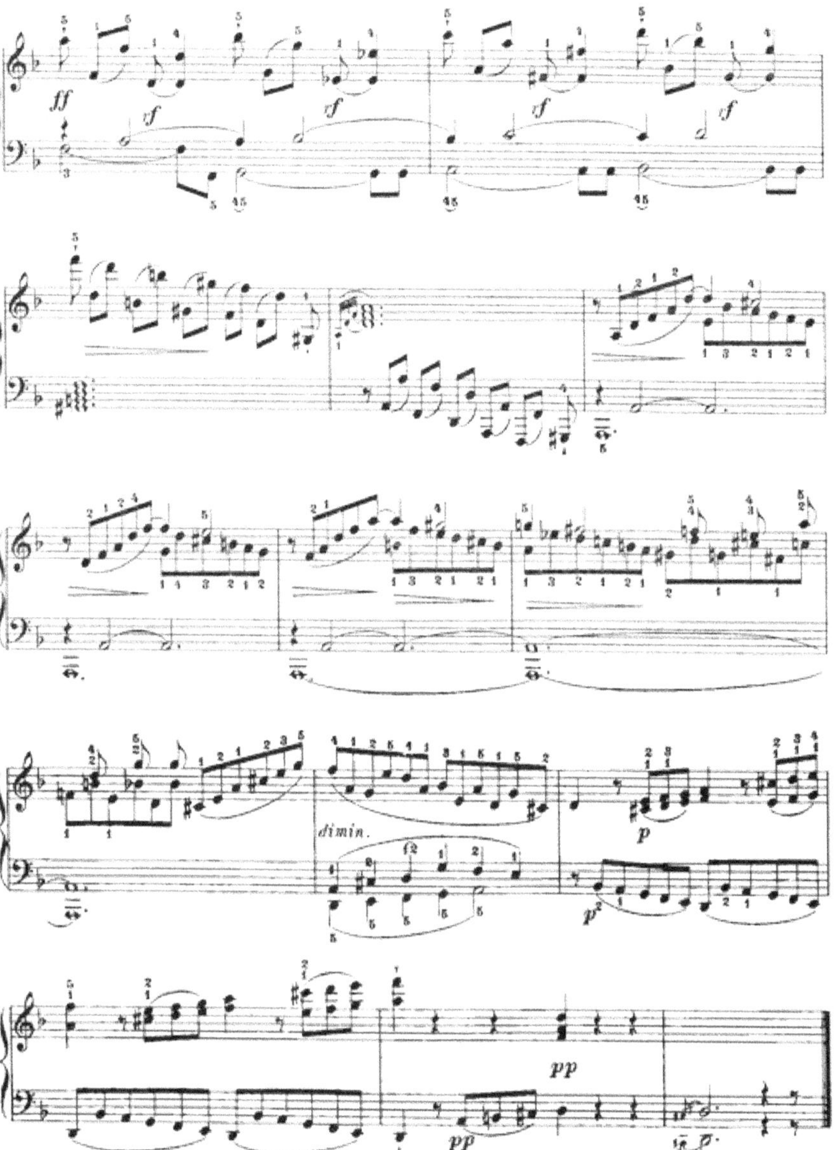
ff
sf
sf
sf
sf
dimin.
p
p
pp
pp

15. Maestoso. (♩ = 76.)

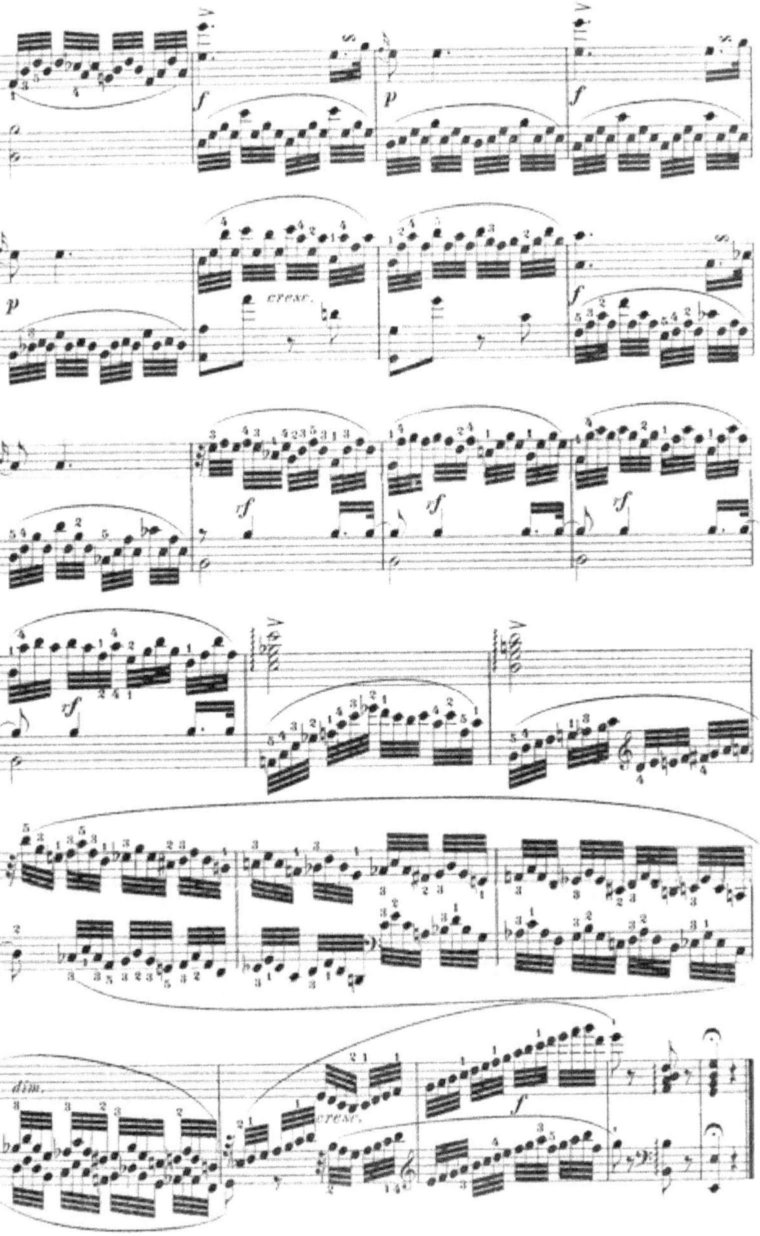

cresc.
dim.
cresc.

Moderato con espressione. (♩= 132.)

16.

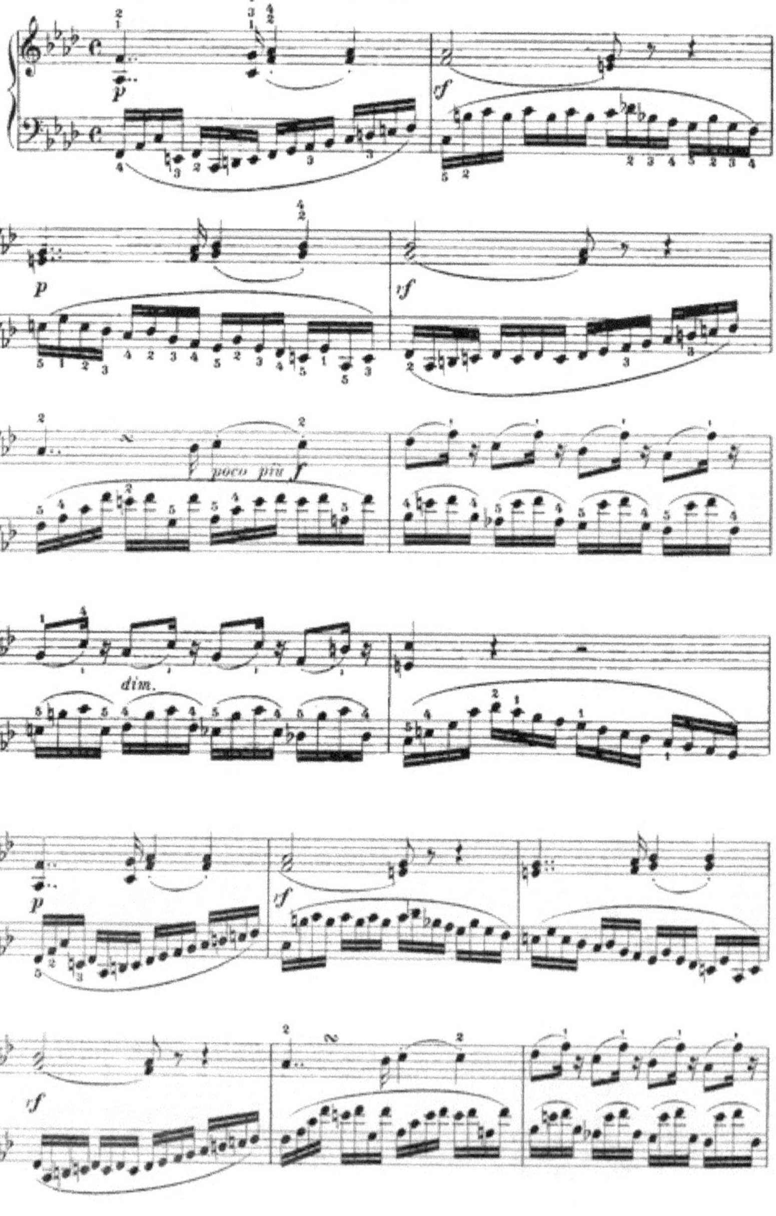

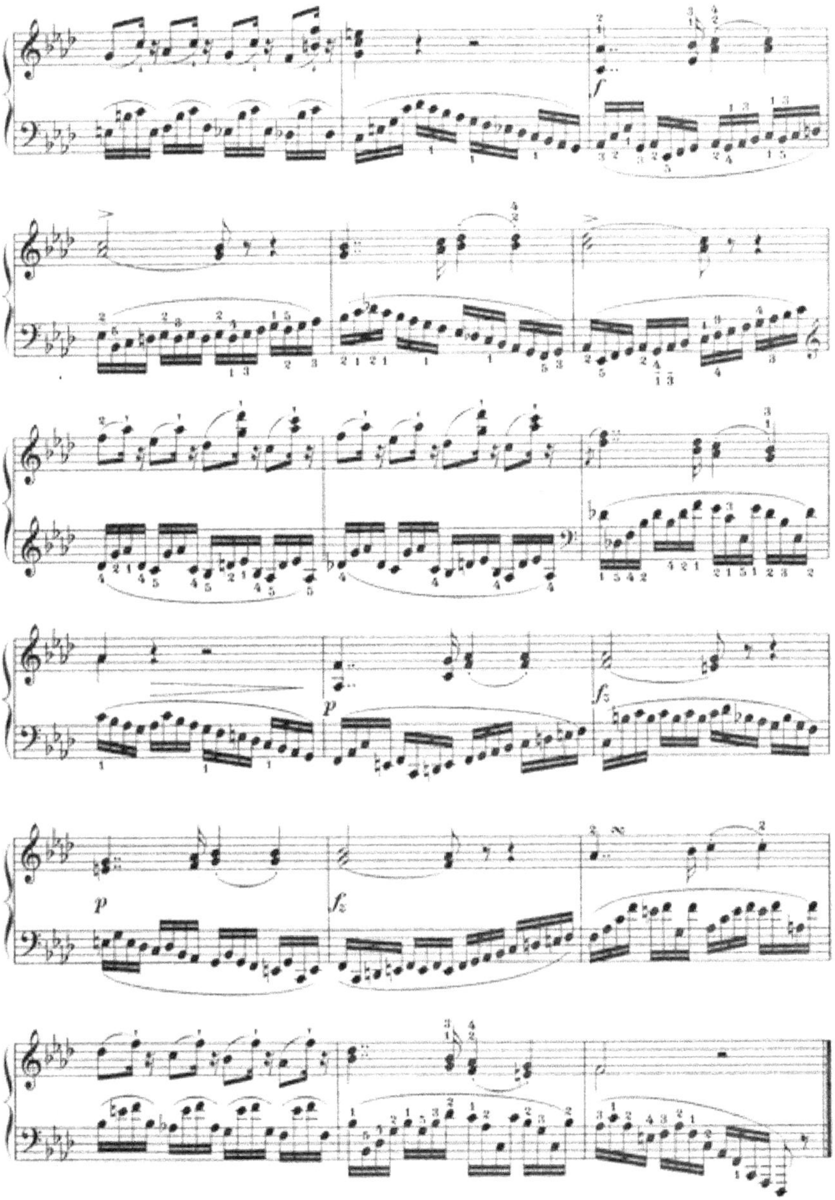

Grazioso, con delicatezza. (♩ = 120.)

17.

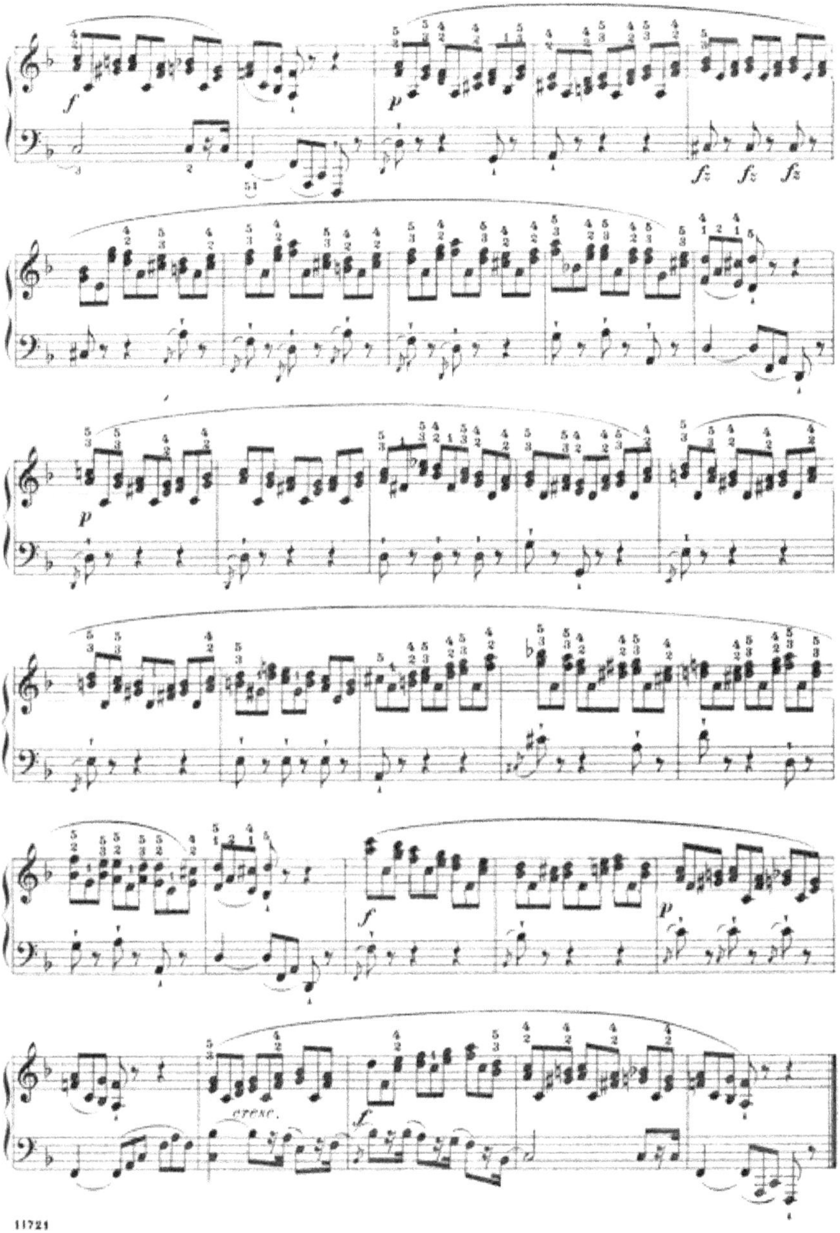
cresc.

18. Allegro. (♪ : 138.)

f *sempre legato*

dimin.

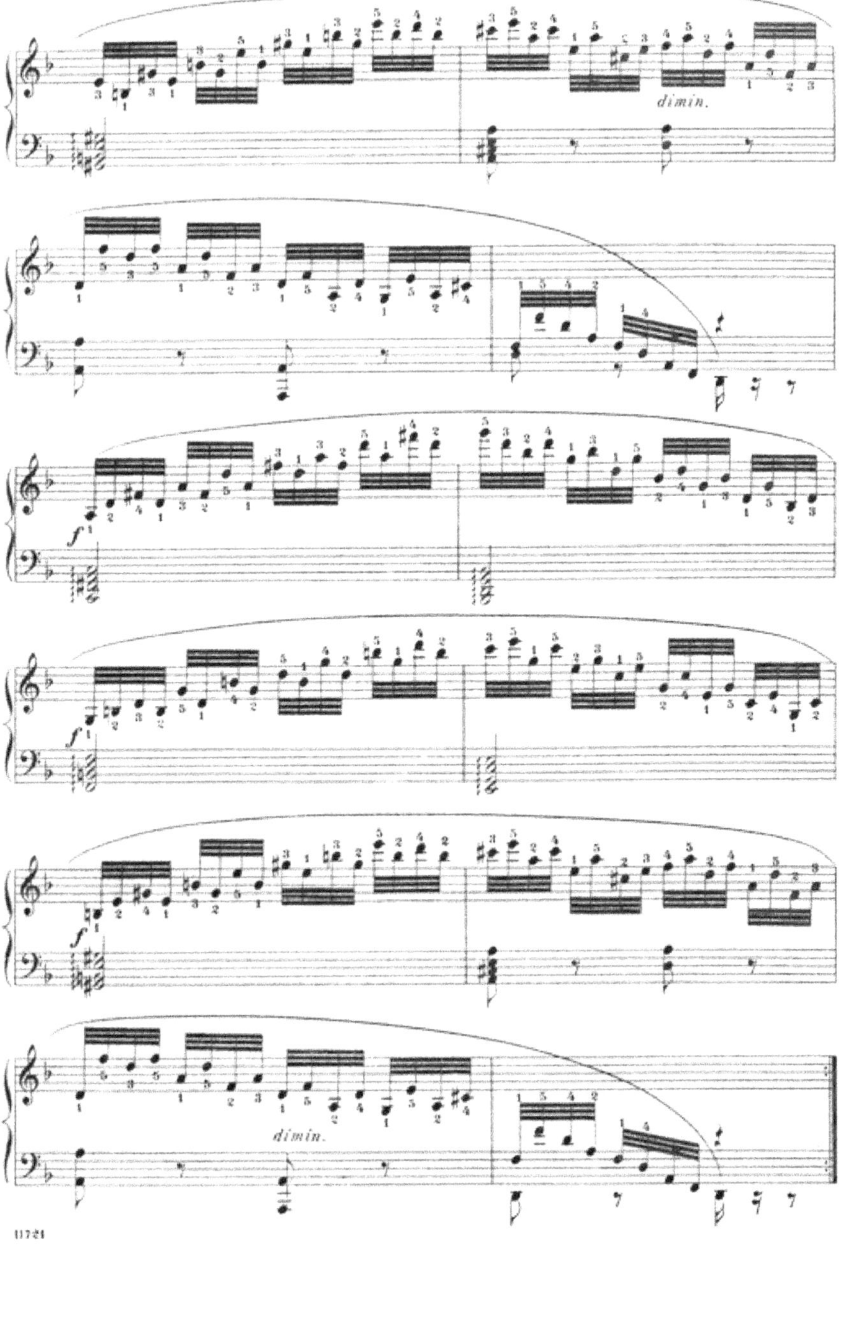
dimin.
f
f
f
dimin.

Allegro con brio. (♩=88.)

19.

legato

fz

fz

cresc.

m.s.

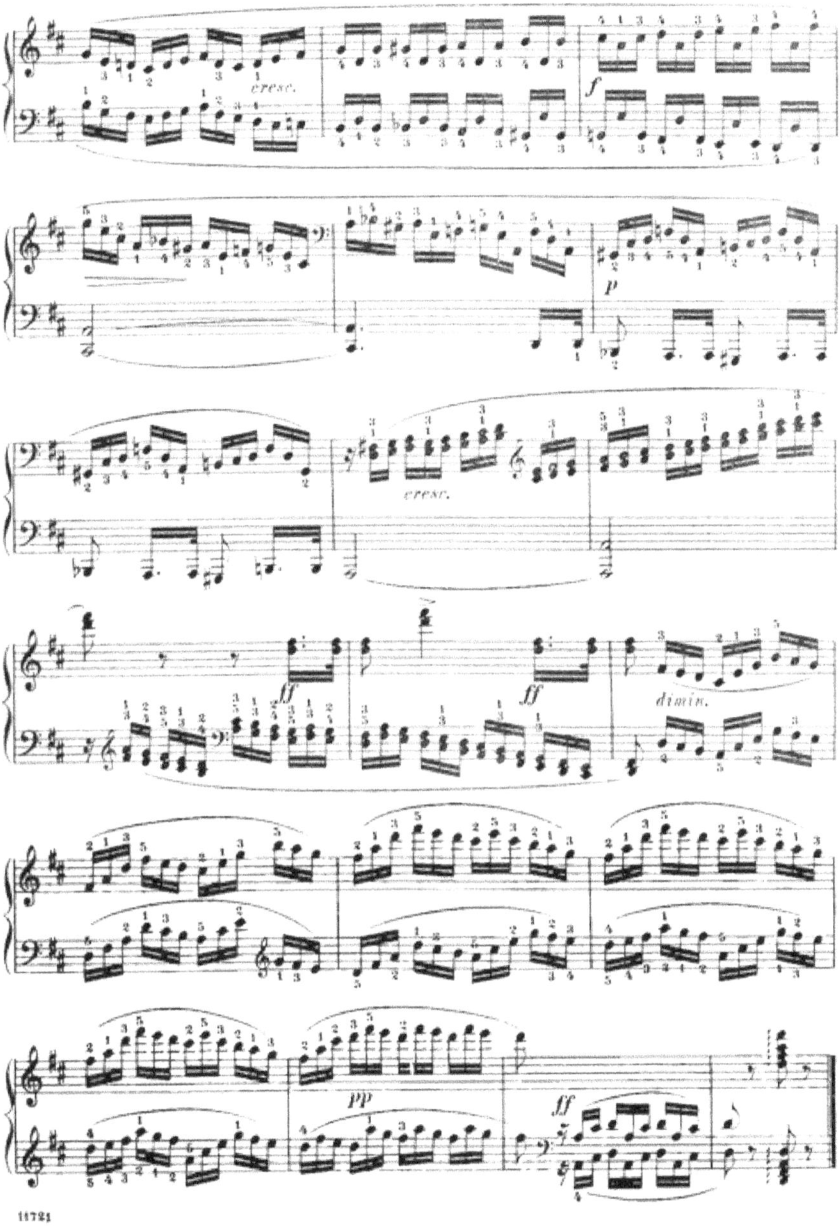
cresc.
f
p
cresc.
ff
ff
dimin.
pp
ff

Con moto. (♩ = 88)

20.

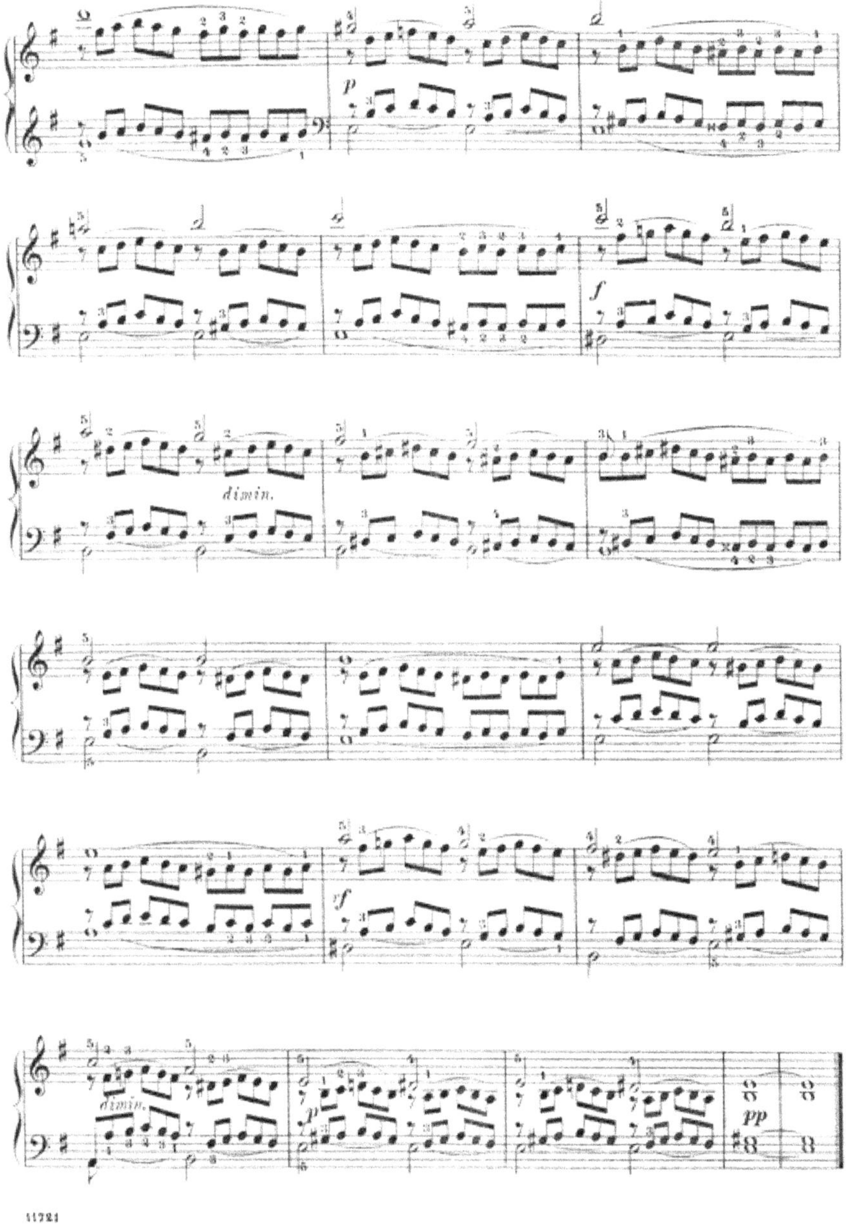
p
f
dimin.
sf
dimin.
pp
pp

42

21.

11781

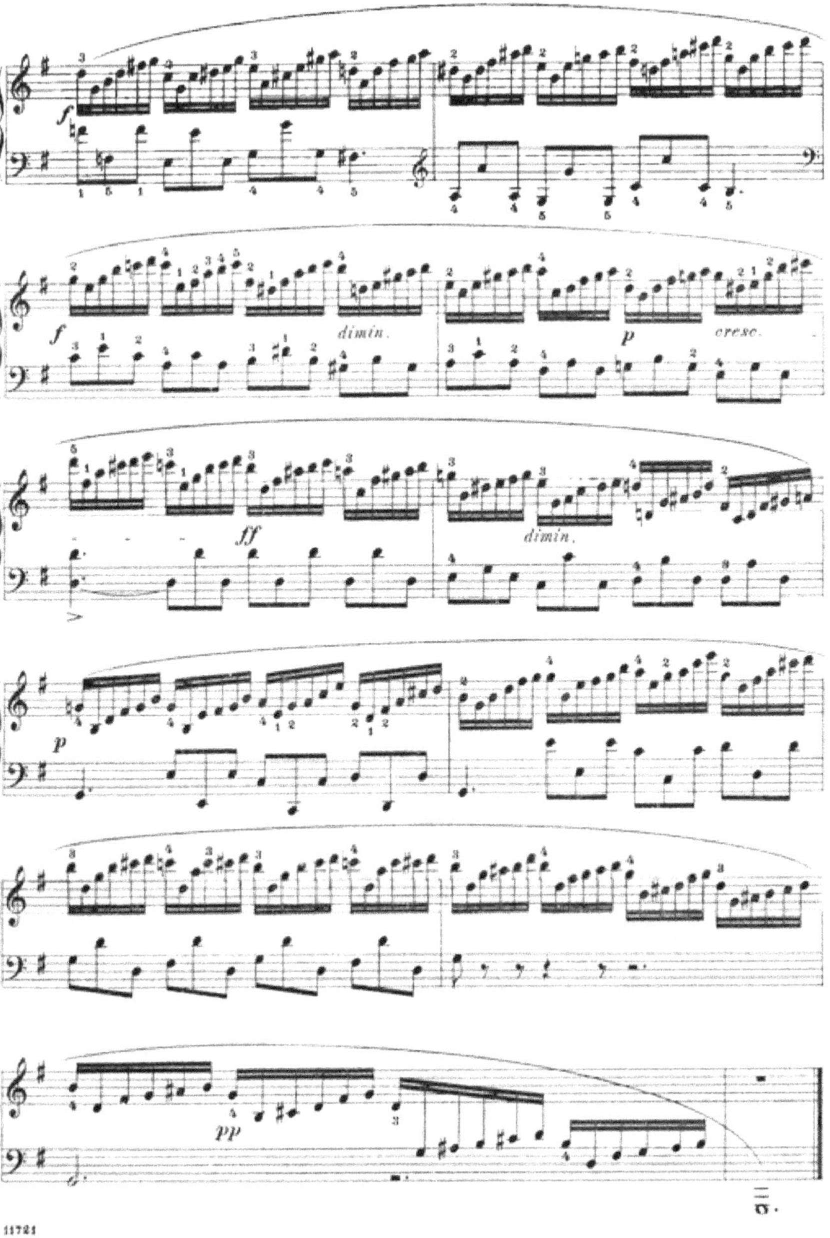
f
f
dimin.
p
cresc.
ff
dimin.
p
pp

SCHIRMER'S LIBRARY
of MUSICAL CLASSICS
EXERCISES AND STUDIES FOR PIANO

Volumes Marked (†) may be obtained in Cloth Binding. Prices will be quoted on request.
A Complete Catalog of Schirmer's Library of Musical Classics will be mailed if desired.

A 542
Published by   **G. SCHIRMER**   New York

SCHIRMER'S SCHOLASTIC SERIES

"Material for vocal and instrumental Study—from the very easiest to the most difficult."

THIS great Series of Books, devoted as the name implies to works of an educational character, is being magnificently received by the musical people all over the country.

The Series embraces only copyrighted works, and contains material covering practically the entire range of instrumental and vocal study.

Many of these works are, and will be, thoroughly original in subject and presentation; while those not strictly novel will always be found superior in point of scope and construction to any existent writing on the same or similar subjects.

New and important works will appear regularly; and in the not distant future **Schirmer's Scholastic Series** will be as well known as the world-famous *Schirmer's Library*.

Several important works previously issued in a different series or character also have been incorporated in this Series.

When ordering ask for *Schirmer's Scholastic Series* (or S. S. S.), and give only the number.

PIANO SOLO

Vol.
74. BECKER, RENÉ L., Five Staccato Études
14. ——10 Melodious Studies. Op. 51
83. BILBRO, MATHILDE, Melodies in minors
89. ——Two Friends (Right and left hand)
39. COERNE, LOUIS ADOLPHE, Eight Studies for the Development of Style
51. DILLER, ANGELA, and QUAILE, ELIZABETH, First Solo Book
72. ——Second Solo Book
105. ——Third Solo Book
13. DOENHOFF, ALBERT VON, 6 Advanced Special Studies Adapted to Small Hands
12. ——3 Modern Piano Études
41. FALCKE, HENRI, School of Arpeggios
30. HUSS, GEORGE J., and HENRY H., Condensed Piano Technic
63. KINSCELLA, HAZEL GERTRUDE, First Steps for the Young Pianist
84. ——Second Steps for the Young Pianist
110. ——Third Steps for the Young Pianist
100. ——Essentials of Piano Technic
1. KRONKE, EMIL, Advanced Studies in Rhythm. Op. 129
17. ——12 Melodic Studies. Medium Grade, Op. 128
9. LEVEY, HENRY, The Chopin Technic
10. LIEBLING, EMIL, The Complete Scales with Explanatory Notes. Op. 13
80. MORA, FLORA, Método moderno de piano para principiantes
PHILIPP, I., Exercises for Independence of the Fingers:
49. ——Part I
50. ——Part II
68. ——School of Octave Playing for Piano, Book I
69. ——The same, Book II
70. ——The same, Book III

A548

Vol.
108. REINHARDT, JACOB, Eight Études for the Development of the 4th and 5th fingers
ROGERS, JAMES H., Development of Velocity. Op. 40. 2 books:
5. ——Book I. Scales
6. ——Book II. Arpeggios
18. ——10 Études
71. ——15 Exercises and Études on Broken Chords
7. ——10 Octave Studies
60. SMITH, HANNAH, 20 Progressive Pedal Studies
31. SPENCER, VERNON, 6 Poetic Study Pieces for Children
65. ——Poetic Studies in Tone Production, Part I
66. ——The same, Part II
67. ——The same, Part III
48 STILLMAN, LOUIS, Concentration and Key-board Facility
38. STERNBERG, CONSTANTIN, Studies in Repetition Technique
WHITING, ARTHUR, Pianoforte Pedal Studies. 2 parts:
19. ——Part I
20. ——Part II
43. WILLIAMS, FREDERICK A., Octave and Chord Studies
42. ——Wrist and Forearm Studies in third, sixths and octaves
16. WRIGHT, N. LOUISE, 12 Études
15. ——12 Preludes

PIANO FOUR-HANDS

52. DILLER, ANGELA, and QUAILE, ELIZABETH, First Duet Book
73. ——Second Duet Book
106. ——Third Duet Book

Diller-Quaile Books

For Piano

By Angela Diller *and* Elizabeth Quaile

This Series has two objects:

(1) To provide, in the earliest stages of the child's piano study, material of permanent musical value which shall serve as a basis for the development of his taste.

With the exception of a few preliminary exercises, all the pieces in the series are either folk-tunes that have been sung by generations of children, or classics that should be part of every child's musical experience.

Music of this character cannot be heard too often, and we feel sure that the teacher as well as the pupil will appreciate the absence of original "teaching pieces."

(2) To provide a plentiful selection of pieces of real musical interest so carefully graded, both musically and technically, that the child is stimulated but not overtaxed.

The pieces are printed only in the more common major and minor keys, but the child should be taught to transpose the pieces into all keys. This insures a familiarity with the keyboard and a sense of tone-relationship that is invaluable.

The four books of duets are graded so as to be used in conjunction with the four books of solos—although each set is complete in itself.

FIRST SOLO BOOK
(Scholastic Series, Vol. 51)
SECOND SOLO BOOK
(Scholastic Series, Vol. 72)
THIRD SOLO BOOK
(Scholastic Series, Vol. 105)
FOURTH SOLO BOOK
(Scholastic Series, Vol. 116) (To be published)

FIRST DUET BOOK
(Scholastic Series, Vol. 52)
SECOND DUET BOOK
(Scholastic Series, Vol. 73)
THIRD DUET BOOK
(Scholastic Series, Vol. 106)
FOURTH DUET BOOK
(Scholastic Series, Vol. 117) (To be published)

Now in constant use by many of the leading teachers, schools and colleges

---

DUET ALBUMS FOR TWO
BEGINNERS IN PIANO PLAYING

First Album, Thirty Folk-Tunes   ARRANGED BY **ANGELA DILLER**

Texts by KATE STEARNS PAGE

THESE are duets in the very simplest form, each number being preceded by the original folk-verses, or a translation of the original. The wholesomeness of the folk-tune principle in early pianoforte study has been amply established, and we offer this volume assured that it will meet with instant success. Large notes, meticulous phrasing, equal difficulty of parts, and "alternating hands" melody-playing are its features beside the main point. Of special importance are the novel marks to indicate *legato, staccato* and *portamento*, respectively. These consist of slurs, dots and inverted brackets presented in an entirely original manner; and they virtually correspond, so used, to commas as found in ordinary English punctuation. The value of these innovations may be estimated by remembering that an inexperienced beginner usually reads from bar to bar, irrespective of the grouping of the piece.

SCHIRMER'S LIBRARY
of MUSICAL CLASSICS
EXERCISES AND STUDIES FOR THE PIANO

V in text ma ed (†) may be obtained in Cloth Binding.   Prices will be quoted on request.
A complete Catalog of Schirmer's Library of Musical Classics will be mailed if desired.

Published by   **G. SCHIRMER**   New York